ANIMALS
BACKPACKS

LEISURE ARTS, INC. • Maumelle, Arkansas

8 PALS TO CROCHET

4

10

15

20

26

30

36

40

Pack some fun in a wildlife backpack! Easy to make with medium weight yarns, you will enjoy creating a pal for that special child in your life.

Meet the Designer: Kristi Simpson

Inspired by her love of yarn, Kristi Simpson creates crochet and knit patterns with a fresh and modern touch. The mother of five became hooked on crochet after teaching herself so she could help her daughter make a scarf from a "learn to crochet" kit that was a gift.

"I loved it from the beginning," she says. "I was amazed that I could take a string of yarn and create something so useful and pretty! Needless to say, I never stopped!"

Look for other Leisure Arts books featuring Kristi's designs at www.leisurearts.com/meet-the-designers/kristi-simpson.html.

●●○○ EASY

Finished Size:
15⅜" wide x 10" deep
(39 cm x 25.5 cm)

GIRAFFE

Giraffe
SHOPPING LIST

Yarn (Medium Weight)
[7 ounces, 370 yards
(198 grams, 338 meters) per skein]:
- ☐ Gold - 1 skein
- ☐ Brown - 1 skein
- ☐ Off White - 20 yards
  (18.5 meters)
- ☐ Black - 10 yards (9 meters)
- ☐ White - small amount

Crochet Hook
- ☐ Size H (5 mm)
  or size needed for gauge

Additional Supplies
- ☐ ⅝" (16 mm) hook-and-loop
  fastener circles - 2
- ☐ Polyester fiberfill
- ☐ Permanent fabric glue
- ☐ Yarn needle

GAUGE INFORMATION
13 sc and 13 rows = 4" (10 cm)
Gauge Swatch: 4" (10 cm) square
With Gold, ch 14.
Row 1: Sc in second ch from hook
and in each ch across: 13 sc.
Rows 2-13: Ch 1, turn; sc in each sc
across.
Finish off.

STITCH GUIDE
SINGLE CROCHET 2 TOGETHER
(abbreviated sc2tog)
Pull up a loop in each of next 2 sts,
YO and draw through all 3 loops on
hook (**counts as one sc**).
DOUBLE CROCHET 2 TOGETHER
(abbreviated dc2tog)
(uses next 2 sts)
★ YO, insert hook in **next** st, YO and
pull up a loop, YO and draw through
2 loops on hook; repeat from ★
once **more**, YO and draw through all
3 loops on hook (**counts as one dc**).

BASE
With Gold, ch 36.

Row 1 (Right side)**:** Sc in second ch
from hook and in each ch across: 35 sc.

Note: Loop a short piece of yarn
around any stitch to mark Row 1 as
right side.

Rows 2-15: Ch 1, turn; sc in each sc
across.

Do **not** finish off.

BODY
Rnd 1: Ch 1, do **not** turn; sc in end
of each row across; working in free
loops of beginning ch *(Fig. 2b,
page 46)*, sc in each ch across; sc in
end of each row across; sc in each
sc across Row 15; join with slip st
to Back Loop Only of first sc *(Fig. 1,
page 46)*: 100 sc.

Rnd 2: Ch 1, sc in Back Loop Only
of same st as joining and each sc
around; join with slip st to **both** loops
of first sc.

Rnd 3: Ch 1, sc in both loops of same
st as joining and in each sc around;
do **not** join, place marker to indicate
beginning of rnd *(see Markers,
page 46)*.

Rnds 4-30: Sc in each sc around; at
end of Rnd 30, slip st in next sc.

Rnd 31: Ch 1, sc in same st as slip st
and in next 7 sc, sc2tog, (sc in next
8 sc, sc2tog) around; join with slip st
to first sc: 90 sc.

Rnd 32: Ch 1, sc in same st as joining
and in next 6 sc, sc2tog, (sc in next
7 sc, sc2tog) around; join with slip st
to first sc: 80 sc.

Rnd 33: Ch 1, sc in same st as joining
and in each sc around; join with
slip st to first sc.

Trim: With **right** side facing, join Gold with slip st in marked st, remove marker; sc in end of each row across Flap to last row, skip last row; beginning in first sc on last row, sc2tog, sc in next 4 sc, place marker in last sc made for Muzzle placement, sc in next sc and in each sc across to last 2 sc, sc2tog; skip first row, sc in end of each row across; slip st in same st as last sc on Row 1 of Flap, finish off.

EYE (Make 2)

Rnd 1 (Right side)**:** With Black, ch 2, 5 sc in second ch from hook; join with slip st to first sc.

Note: Mark Rnd 1 as **right** side.

Rnd 2: Ch 1, 2 sc in same st as joining and in each sc around; join with slip st to first sc, finish off leaving a long end for sewing.

Using photo as a guide for placement, with White and straight stitch *(Fig. 5, page 47)*, add highlight to each Eye.

Rnd 34: Ch 1, sc in same st as joining and in next 5 sc, sc2tog, (sc in next 6 sc, sc2tog) around; join with slip st to first sc: 70 sc.

Rnds 35-37: Ch 1, sc in same st as joining and in each sc around; join with slip st to first sc.

Rnd 38: Ch 1, sc in same st as joining and in next 19 sc, place marker in last sc made for Flap and Trim placement, sc in each sc around; join with slip st in first sc, finish off.

FLAP

Row 1: With **right** side facing and working in Back Loops Only, join Gold with sc in marked st *(see Joining With Sc, page 46)*; do **not** remove marker, sc in next 29 sc, leave remaining sc unworked: 30 sc.

Rows 2-20: Ch 1, turn; sc in both loops of each sc across.

Rows 21 and 22: Turn; beginning in first sc, sc2tog, sc in each sc across to last 2 sc, sc2tog: 26 sc.

Finish off.

HORN (Make 2)

Rnd 1 (Right side): With Brown, ch 2, 4 sc in second ch from hook; do **not** join, place marker to indicate beginning of rnd.

Note: Mark Rnd 1 as **right** side.

Rnd 2: 2 Sc in each sc around: 8 sc.

Rnd 3: (Sc in next sc, 2 sc in next sc) around: 12 sc.

Rnds 4 and 5: Sc in each sc around.

Rnd 6: (Sc in next sc, sc2tog) around; slip st in next sc, finish off: 8 sc.

Rnd 7: With **right** side facing, join Gold with sc in any sc; sc in each sc around; join with slip st to first sc.

Rnds 8-11: Ch 1, sc in same st as joining and in each sc around; join with slip st to first sc.

Finish off leaving a long end for sewing.

Stuff Horn with polyester fiberfill.

EAR (Make 2)

Rnd 1 (Right side): With Gold, ch 4, 5 dc in fourth ch from hook; skip beginning ch and join with slip st to first dc: 5 dc.

Note: Mark Rnd 1 as **right** side.

Rnd 2: Ch 2 (**does not count as a st, now and throughout**), 2 dc in same st as joining and in each dc around; join with slip st to first dc: 10 dc.

Rnd 3: Ch 2, dc in same st as joining, 2 dc in next dc, (dc in next dc, 2 dc in next dc) around; join with slip st to first dc: 15 dc.

Rnd 4: Ch 2, dc in same st as joining and in each dc around; join with slip st to first dc.

Rnd 5: Ch 2, dc in same st as joining, dc2tog, (dc in next dc, dc2tog) around; join with slip st to first dc: 10 dc.

Rnd 6: Ch 2, dc in same st as joining and in next dc, dc2tog, (dc in next dc, dc2tog) twice; join with slip st to first dc, finish off leaving a long end for sewing: 7 dc.

SMALL SPOTS (Make 3)

With Brown, ch 7.

Row 1 (Right side): Dc in fourth ch from hook and in each ch across: 5 sts.

Note: Mark Row 1 as **right** side.

Row 2: Ch 3 (**counts as first dc, now and throughout**), turn; dc in next dc and in each st across.

Trim: Ch 1, turn; 3 sc in first dc, sc in next 3 dc, 3 sc in last dc; 2 sc in end of each row across; working in free loops of beginning ch, 3 sc in first ch, sc in next 3 chs, 3 sc in next ch; 2 sc in end of each row across; join with slip st to first sc, finish off leaving a long end for sewing.

MEDIUM SPOTS (Make 5)

With Brown, ch 10.

Row 1 (Right side): Dc in fourth ch from hook and in each ch across: 8 sts.

Note: Mark Row 1 as **right** side.

Rows 2 and 3: Ch 3, turn; dc in next dc and in each st across.

Trim: Ch 1, do **not** turn; 2 sc in end of each row across; working in free loops of beginning ch, 3 sc in first ch, sc in next 6 chs, 3 sc in next ch; 2 sc in end of each row across; 3 sc in first dc, sc in next 6 dc, 3 sc in last dc; join with slip st to first sc, finish off leaving a long end for sewing.

MUZZLE

Row 1: With **right** side facing and working in Front Loops Only *(Fig. 1, page 46)*, join Off White with sc in marked sc on Flap Trim; sc in next 15 sc, leave remaining sc unworked: 16 sc.

Rows 2-7: Ch 1, turn; sc in both loops of each sc across.

Rows 8-11: Ch 1, turn; beginning in first sc, sc2tog, sc across to last 2 sc, sc2tog: 8 sc.

Finish off leaving a long end for sewing.

Sew Muzzle to Flap.
With Brown and using straight stitch, add 'X' nostrils to Muzzle.

STRAP (Make 2)

With Brown, ch 46, place marker in second ch from hook for st placement.

Rnd 1 (Right side)**:** Sc in second ch from hook and in each ch across to last ch, 3 sc in last ch; working in free loops of beginning ch, sc in each ch across to marked ch, 3 sc in marked ch, remove marker; join with slip st to first sc: 94 sc.

Note: Mark Rnd 1 as **right** side.

Rnd 2: Ch 1, sc in same st as joining and in each sc across to first 3-sc group, 3 sc in next sc, sc in next sc, 3 sc in next sc, sc in each sc to next 3-sc group, 3 sc in next sc, sc in next sc, 3 sc in last sc; join with slip st to first sc, finish off leaving a long end for sewing.

FINISHING

Using photo as a guide for placement, long ends and with **right** sides of all pieces facing:

Sew Eyes to Flap.

Sew Horns to Rnd 38 and Rows 1 and 2 of Flap, spaced 2 sc apart on Rnd 38.

Sew Ears to Row 1 of Flap on each side of Horns.

Sew Spots randomly to Body.

Sew short end of each Strap to free loops of sts on Rnd 38 (*Fig. 2a, page 46*), starting 5 sts from each edge of Flap. Sew remaining short end of each Strap to bottom edge of Body.

Glue hook-and-loop fastener circles to **wrong** side corners of Flap and to corresponding areas on Body.

MANE

Cut 13, 4" (10 cm) lengths of Brown.

Fold one strand in half. With **right** side facing and using a crochet hook, draw the folded end around post of any sc on Row 1 of Flap (*Fig. A*) between Horns and pull the loose ends through the folded end; draw the knot up **tightly** (*Fig. B*). Repeat, working around posts of each of four middle sc on Rows 1 and 2 and middle 5 sc on Row 3.

Fig. A

Fig. B

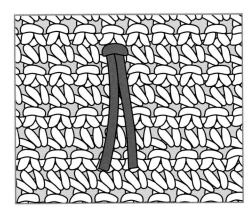

●●○○ **EASY**

Finished Size:
15⅜" wide x 10" deep
(39 cm x 25.5 cm)

SHOPPING LIST

Yarn (Medium Weight) **MEDIUM 4**
[3.5 ounces, 170 yards
(100 grams, 156 meters) per skein]:
☐ Beige - 2 skeins
☐ Brown - 1 skein
☐ Blue - 1 skein
☐ Black - 10 yards (9 meters)
☐ White - small amount

Crochet Hook
☐ Size H (5 mm)
or size needed for gauge

Additional Supplies
☐ ⅝" (16 mm) hook-and-loop
fastener circles - 2
☐ Permanent fabric glue
☐ Yarn needle

LION

Lion

GAUGE INFORMATION

13 sc and 13 rows = 4" (10 cm)

Gauge Swatch: 4" (10 cm) square
With White, ch 14.

Row 1: Sc in second ch from hook
and in each ch across: 13 sc.

Rows 2-13: Ch 1, turn; sc in each sc
across.
Finish off.

STITCH GUIDE

SINGLE CROCHET 2 TOGETHER
  (abbreviated sc2tog)

Pull up a loop in each of next 2 sts,
YO and draw through all 3 loops on
hook **(counts as one sc)**.

BASE

With Beige, ch 36.

Row 1 (Right side): Sc in second ch
from hook and in each ch across:
35 sc.

Note: Loop a short piece of yarn
around any stitch to mark Row 1 as
right side.

Rows 2-15: Ch 1, turn; sc in each sc
across.

Do **not** finish off.

BODY

Rnd 1: Ch 1, do **not** turn; sc in end
of each row across; working in free
loops of beginning ch *(Fig. 2b,
page 46)*, sc in each ch across; sc in
end of each row across; sc in each
sc across Row 15; join with slip st
to Back Loop Only of first sc *(Fig. 1,
page 46)*: 100 sc.

Rnd 2: Ch 1, sc in Back Loop Only
of same at as joining and each sc
around; join with slip st to **both** loops
of first sc.

Rnd 3: Ch 2 **(does not count as a st,
now and throughout)**, dc in same st
as joining and in next 2 sc, ch 1, skip
next sc, ★ dc in next 3 sc, ch 1, skip
next sc; repeat from ★ around; join
with slip st to first dc, finish off: 75 dc
and 25 ch-1 sps.

Rnd 4: With **right** side facing, join
Blue with sc in last ch-1 sp *(see
Joining With Sc, page 46)*; ch 3, (sc in
next ch-1 sp, ch 3) around; join with
slip st to first sc, finish off.

Rnd 5: With **right** side facing, join
Beige with dc in last ch-3 sp *(see
Joining With Dc, page 46)*; 2 dc in
same sp, ch 1, (3 dc in next ch-3 sp,
ch 1) around; join with slip st to first
dc, finish off.

Rnd 6: With **right** side facing, join
Brown with sc in first ch-1 sp; ch 3,
(sc in next ch-1 sp, ch 3) around; join
with slip st to first sc, finish off.

Rnd 7: With **right** side facing, join
Beige with dc in last ch-3 sp; 2 dc in
same sp, ch 1, (3 dc in next ch-3 sp,
ch 1) around; join with slip st to first
dc, finish off.

Rnds 8-19: Repeat Rnds 4-7, 3 times;
at end of Rnd 19, do **not** finish off.

Rnd 20: Ch 1, working in dc and chs,
sc in same st as joining and in next
7 sts, sc2tog, (sc in next 8 sts, sc2tog)
around; join with slip st to first sc:
90 sc.

Rnd 21: Ch 1, sc in same st as joining
and in next 6 sc, sc2tog, (sc in next
7 sc, sc2tog) around; join with slip st
to first sc: 80 sc.

Rnd 22: Ch 1, sc in same st as joining
and in each sc around; join with
slip st to first sc.

Rnd 23: Ch 1, sc in same st as joining
and in next 5 sc, sc2tog, (sc in next
6 sc, sc2tog) around; join with slip st
to first sc: 70 sc.

Rnds 24-26: Ch 1, sc in same st as
joining and in each sc around; join
with slip st to first sc.

Rnd 27: Ch 1, sc in same st as joining and in next 11 sc, place marker in last sc made for Flap and Trim placement, sc in each sc around; join with slip st to first sc, finish off.

FLAP

Row 1: With **right** side facing and working in Back Loops Only, join Beige with sc in marked st; do **not** remove marker, sc in next 29 sc, leave remaining sc unworked, place marker in last sc made for Mane placement: 30 sc.

Rows 2-20: Ch 1, turn; sc in both loops of each sc across.

Rows 21 and 22: Turn; beginning in first sc, sc2tog, sc in each sc across to last 2 sc, sc2tog: 26 sc.

Finish off.

Trim: With **right** side facing, join Beige with slip st in marked st on Rnd 27, remove marker; sc in end of each row across Flap to last row, skip last row; beginning in first sc on last row, sc2tog, sc in each sc across to last 2 sc, sc2tog; skip first row, sc in end of each row across; slip st in same st as last sc on Row 1 of Flap, finish off.

EYE (Make 2)

Rnd 1 (Right side)**:** With Black, ch 2, 5 sc in second ch from hook; join with slip st to first sc.

Note: Mark Rnd 1 as **right** side.

Rnd 2: Ch 1, 2 sc in same st as joining and in each sc around; join with slip st to first sc, finish off leaving a long end for sewing.

Using photo on page 10 as a guide for placement, with White and straight stitch *(Fig. 5, page 47)*, add highlight to each Eye.

NOSE

Row 1: With Brown, ch 2, 2 sc in second ch from hook.

Row 2 (Right side)**:** Ch 1, turn; 2 sc in each sc across: 4 sc.

Note: Mark Row 2 as **right** side.

Row 3: Ch 1, turn; 2 sc in first sc, sc in next 2 sc, 2 sc in last sc: 6 sc.

Rows 4 and 5: Ch 1, turn; sc in each sc across.

Trim: Ch 1, turn; 3 sc in first sc, sc in next 4 sc, 3 sc in last sc; skip first row, sc in end of next 4 rows, 3 sc in free loop of beginning ch; sc in end of next 4 rows, skip last row; join with slip st to first sc, finish off leaving a long end for sewing.

EAR (Make 2)

Rnd 1 (Right side)**:** With Beige, ch 2, 4 sc in second ch from hook; do **not** join, place marker to indicate beginning of rnd *(see Markers, page 46)*.

Rnd 2: 2 Sc in each sc around: 8 sc.

Rnd 3: (Sc in next sc, 2 sc in next sc) around: 12 sc.

Rnds 4-6: Sc in each sc around.

Finish off leaving a long end for sewing.

STRAP (Make 2)

With Blue, ch 46, place marker in second ch from hook for st placement.

Rnd 1 (Right side)**:** Sc in second ch from hook and in each ch across to last ch, 3 sc in last ch; working in free loops of beginning ch, sc in each ch across to marked ch, 3 sc in marked ch, remove marker; join with slip st to first sc: 94 sc.

Note: Mark Rnd 1 as **right** side.

Rnd 2: Ch 1, sc in same st as joining and in each sc across to first 3-sc group, 3 sc in next sc, sc in next sc, 3 sc in next sc, sc in each sc across to next 3-sc group, 3 sc in next sc, sc in next sc, 3 sc in last sc; join with slip st to first sc, finish off leaving a long end for sewing.

FINISHING

Using photo as a guide for placement, long ends, and with **right** sides of all pieces facing:
Sew Eyes to Flap.
Sew Nose to Flap.
With two strands of Brown and using backstitch *(Fig. 3, page 47)*, add mouth below the nose.

Sew short end of each Strap to free loops of sts on Rnd 27 *(Fig. 2a, page 46)*, starting 5 sts from each edge of Flap. Sew remaining short end of each Strap to bottom edge of Body.
Glue hook-and-loop fastener circles to **wrong** side corners of Flap and to corresponding areas on Body.

MANE

Foundation Row: With **right** side of Flap facing and working around posts of sc on Row 1, join Brown with sc around marked sc; remove marker, sc around next 29 sc; do **not** finish off.

Rnd 1: Ch 1, do **not** turn; slip st in Back Loop Only of first sc on Trim, (ch 10, slip st in Back Loop Only of next sc) around Trim and across Foundation Row; do **not** join.

Rnd 2: Ch 1, slip st in free loop of first sc on Trim, (ch 10, slip st in free loop of next sc) around Trim and across Foundation Row; join with slip st to first slip st, finish off.

Sew each Ear at a slight angle across top corners of Flap.

●●○○ EASY

Finished Size:
15⅜" wide x 10" deep
(39 cm x 25.5 cm)

ZEBRA

Zebra

SHOPPING LIST

Yarn (Medium Weight)

[7 ounces, 370 yards
(198 grams, 338 meters) per skein]:

- ☐ Pink - 1 skein
- ☐ White - 1 skein
- ☐ Black - 1 skein

Crochet Hook

- ☐ Size H (5 mm)
  or size needed for gauge

Additional Supplies

- ☐ ⅝" (16 mm) hook-and-loop
  fastener circles - 2
- ☐ Permanent fabric glue
- ☐ Yarn needle

GAUGE INFORMATION

13 sc and 13 rows = 4" (10 cm)

Gauge Swatch: 4" (10 cm) square
With Pink, ch 14.

Row 1: Sc in second ch from hook
and in each ch across: 13 sc.

Rows 2-13: Ch 1, turn; sc in each sc
across.

Finish off.

STITCH GUIDE

SINGLE CROCHET 2 TOGETHER

(abbreviated sc2tog)

Pull up a loop in each of next 2 sts,
YO and draw through all 3 loops on
hook (**counts as one sc**).

DOUBLE CROCHET 2 TOGETHER

(abbreviated dc2tog)

(uses next 2 sts)

★ YO, insert hook in **next** dc, YO and
pull up a loop, YO and draw through
2 loops on hook; repeat from ★
once **more**, YO and draw through all
3 loops on hook (**counts as one dc**).

LONG SC (abbreviated LSC)

Insert hook in st indicated, YO and
pull up a loop even with last st made,
YO and draw through both loops on
hook.

BASE

With Pink, ch 36.

Row 1 (Right side)**:** Sc in second ch
from hook and in each ch across:
35 sc.

Note: Loop a short piece of yarn
around any stitch to mark Row 1 as
right side.

Rows 2-15: Ch 1, turn; sc in each sc
across.

Do **not** finish off.

BODY

Rnd 1: Ch 1, do **not** turn; sc in end
of each row across; working in free
loops of beginning ch (*Fig. 2b,
page 46*), sc in each ch across; sc in
end of each row across; sc in each
sc across Row 15; join with slip st
to Back Loop Only of first sc (*Fig. 1,
page 46*): 100 sc.

Rnd 2: Ch 1, sc in Back Loop Only
of same st as joining and each sc
around; join with slip st to **both** loops
of first sc.

Rnd 3: Ch 1, sc in both loops of same
st as joining and in each sc around;
do **not** join, place marker to indicate
beginning of rnd (*see Markers,
page 46*).

Rnds 4-6: Sc in each sc around;
at end of Rnd 6, slip st in next sc,
finish off.

Rnd 7: With **right** side facing, join
Black with dc in same st as slip st (*see
Joining With Dc, page 46*); dc in same
st, skip next sc, (2 dc in next sc, skip
next sc) around; join with slip st to
first dc, finish off.

Rnd 8: With **right** side facing, join White with dc in sp **between** first 2 dc *(Fig. A)*; dc in same sp, skip next 2 dc, ★ 2 dc in sp **before** next dc, skip next 2 dc; repeat from ★ around; join with slip st to first dc, finish off.

Fig. A

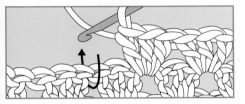

Rnd 9: With **right** side facing, join Black with dc in sp **between** first 2 dc; dc in same sp, skip next 2 dc, ★ 2 dc in sp **before** next dc, skip next 2 dc; repeat from ★ around; join with slip st to first dc, finish off.

Rnds 10-21: Repeat Rnds 8 and 9, 6 times; at end of Rnd 21, do **not** finish off.

Rnd 22: Ch 1, sc in same st as joining and in next 7 dc, sc2tog, (sc in next 8 dc, sc2tog) around; join with slip st to first sc: 90 sc.

Rnd 23: Ch 1, sc in same st as joining and in next 6 sc, sc2tog, (sc in next 7 sc, sc2tog) around; join with slip st to first sc: 80 sc.

Rnd 24: Ch 1, sc in same st as joining and in each sc around; join with slip st to first sc.

Rnd 25: Ch 1, sc in same st as joining and in next 5 sc, sc2tog, (sc in next 6 sc, sc2tog) around; join with slip st to first sc: 70 sc.

Rnds 26 and 27: Ch 1, sc in same st as joining and in each sc around; join with slip st to first sc.

Finish off.

Rnd 28: With **right** side facing, join Pink with sc in same st *(see Joining With Sc, page 46)*; sc in each sc around; join with slip st to first sc.

Rnd 29: Ch 1, sc in same st as joining and in next 45 sc, place marker in last sc made for Flap and Trim placement, sc in each sc around; join with slip st to first sc, finish off.

FLAP

Row 1: With **right** side facing and working in Back Loops Only, join White with sc in marked st; do **not** remove marker, sc in next 29 sc, leave remaining sc unworked: 30 sc.

Rows 2-20: Ch 1, turn; sc in both loops of each sc across.

Rows 21 and 22: Turn; beginning in first sc, sc2tog, sc in each sc across to last 2 sc, sc2tog: 26 sc.

Finish off.

Trim: With **right** side facing, join Black with slip st in marked st on Rnd 29, remove marker; † working in ends of rows on Flap, skip first row, sc in next row, work LSC in second sc of next row, (work LSC in third sc of next row, work LSC in second sc of next row) 9 times, skip last row †; beginning in first sc, sc2tog, place marker in st just made for Muzzle placement, sc in each sc across to last 2 sc, sc2tog; repeat from † to † across, slip st in same st as last sc on Row 1 of Flap, finish off.

EYE (Make 2)

Rnd 1 (Right side)**:** With Black, ch 2, 5 sc in second ch from hook; join with slip st to first sc.

Note: Mark Rnd 1 as **right** side.

Rnd 2: Ch 1, 2 sc in same st as joining and in each sc around; join with slip st to first sc, finish off leaving a long end for sewing.

Using photo on page 15 as a guide for placement, with White and straight stitch *(Fig. 5, page 47)*, add highlight to each Eye.

MUZZLE

Row 1: With **right** side facing and working in Front Loops Only *(Fig. 1, page 46)*, join Black with sc in marked sc on Trim, remove marker; sc in next 23 sc, leave remaining sc unworked: 24 sc.

Rows 2-5: Ch 1, turn, sc in both loops of each sc across.

Rows 6-10: Ch 1, turn; sc in first sc, sc2tog, sc in each sc across to last 3 sc, sc2tog, sc in last sc: 14 sc.

Row 11: Ch 1, turn; beginning in first sc, sc2tog, sc in each sc across to last 2 sc, sc2tog; finish off leaving a long end for sewing.

Sew Muzzle to Flap.

With Pink and using straight stitch, add 'X' nostrils to Muzzle.

EAR (Make 2)

Rnd 1 (Right side)**:** With Black, ch 4, 3 dc in fourth ch from hook; skip beginning ch and join with slip st to first dc: 3 dc.

Note: Mark Rnd 1 as **right** side.

Rnd 2: Ch 2 **(does not count as a st, now and throughout)**, 2 dc in same st as joining and in each dc around; join with slip st to first dc: 6 dc.

Rnd 3: Ch 2, 2dc in same st as joining and in each dc around; join with slip st to first dc: 12 dc.

Rnd 4: Ch 2, dc in same st as joining, 2 dc in next dc, (dc in next dc, 2 dc in next dc) around; join with slip st to first dc: 18 dc.

Rnds 5 and 6: Ch 2, dc in same st as joining and in each dc around; join with slip st to first dc.

Rnds 7 and 8: Ch 2, dc in same st as joining, dc2tog, (dc in next dc, dc2tog) around; join with slip st to first dc, finish off leaving a long end for sewing: 8 dc.

STRAP (Make 2)

With Pink, ch 46, place marker in second ch from hook for st placement.

Rnd 1 (Right side)**:** Sc in second ch from hook and in each ch across to last ch, 3 sc in last ch; working in free loops of beginning ch, sc in each ch across to marked ch, 3 sc in marked ch, remove marker; join with slip st to first sc: 94 sc.

Note: Mark Rnd 1 as **right** side.

Rnd 2: Ch 1, sc in same st as joining and in each sc across to first 3-sc group, 3 sc in next sc, sc in next sc, 3 sc in next sc, sc in each sc across to next 3-sc group, 3 sc in next sc, sc in next sc, 3 sc in last sc; join with slip st to first sc, finish off leaving a long end for sewing.

FINISHING

Using photo as a guide for placement, long ends, and with **right** sides of all pieces facing:
Sew Eyes and Ears to Flap.
Sew short end of each Strap to free loops of sts on Rnd 29 *(Fig. 2a, page 46)*, starting 5 sts from each edge of Flap. Sew remaining short end of each Strap to bottom edge of Body.
Glue hook-and-loop fastener circles to **wrong** side corners of Flap and to corresponding areas on Body.

MANE

Cut 20, 4" (10 cm) lengths of Pink. Fold two strands in half. With **right** side facing and using a crochet hook, draw the folded end around post of middle sc on Row 29 (between Straps) and pull the loose ends through the folded end; draw the knot up **tightly** *(Figs. A & B, page 21)*. Repeat, working around next two sc on each side of middle sc.

Fold two strands in half. With **right** side facing, using a crochet hook and working in free loops of each sc previously worked around, draw the folded end up through a stitch and pull the loose ends through the folded end *(Fig. B)*; draw the knot up **tightly** *(Fig. C)*. Repeat in remaining sc worked around.

Fig. B

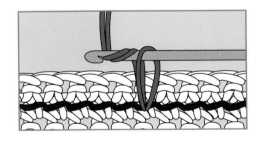

Fig. C

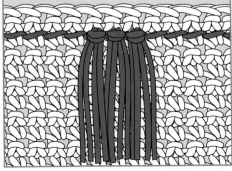

Finished Size:
15⅜" wide x 10" deep
(39 cm x 25.5 cm)

SHOPPING LIST

Yarn (Medium Weight)

[7 ounces, 370 yards
(198 grams, 338 meters) per skein]:

☐ Yellow - 1 skein

☐ Black - 1 skein

☐ White - 1 skein

Crochet Hook

☐ Size H (5 mm)

or size needed for gauge

Additional Supplies

☐ Safety pin

☐ ⅝" (16 mm) hook-and-loop
fastener circles - 2

☐ Permanent fabric glue

☐ Yarn needle

BEE

Bee

GAUGE INFORMATION

13 sc and 13 rows = 4" (10 cm)

Gauge Swatch: 4" (10 cm) square
With White, ch 14.

Row 1: Sc in second ch from hook and in each ch across: 13 sc.

Rows 2-13: Ch 1, turn; sc in each sc across.
Finish off.

STITCH GUIDE

SINGLE CROCHET 2 TOGETHER
(abbreviated sc2tog)

Pull up a loop in each of next 2 sts, YO and draw through all 3 loops on hook (**counts as one sc**).

BASE

With Black, ch 36.

Row 1 (Right side)**:** Sc in second ch from hook and in each ch across: 35 sc.

Note: Loop a short piece of yarn around any stitch to mark Row 1 as **right** side.

Rows 2-15: Ch 1, turn; sc in each sc across.

Do **not** finish off.

BODY

Rnd 1: Ch 1, do **not** turn; sc in end of each row across; working in free loops of beginning ch (*Fig. 2b, page 46*), sc in each ch across; sc in end of each row across; sc in each sc across Row 15; join with slip st to first sc, finish off: 100 sc.

Rnd 2: With **right** side facing and working in Back Loops Only (*Fig. 1, page 46*), join Yellow with dc in same st as joining (*see Joining With Dc, page 46*); dc in next sc and in each sc around; join with slip st to **both** loops of first dc.

Rnd 3: Ch 2 (**does not count as a st, now and throughout**), dc in same st as joining and in each dc around; join with slip st to first dc, place loop from hook onto safety pin to keep piece from unraveling while working the next rnd.

Rnd 4: With **right** side facing, join Black with slip st in same st as joining; **loosely** slip st in each dc around; join with slip st to first slip st, finish off.

Rnd 5: Remove loop from safety pin and place on hook. Ch 2, working in dc of previous rnd, dc in same st as joining and in each dc around; join with slip st to first dc.

Rnd 6: Ch 2, dc in same st as joining and in each dc around; join with slip st to first dc, place loop from hook onto safety pin to keep piece from unraveling while working the next rnd.

Rnds 7-20: Repeat Rnds 4-6, 4 times; then repeat Rnds 4 and 5 once **more**.

Rnd 21: Ch 1, sc in same st as joining and in next 7 dc, sc2tog, (sc in next 8 dc, sc2tog) around; join with slip st to first sc: 90 sc.

Rnd 22: Ch 1, sc in same st as joining and in next 6 sc, sc2tog, (sc in next 7 sc, sc2tog) around; join with slip st to first sc: 80 sc.

Rnd 23: Ch 1, sc in same st as joining and in each sc around; join with slip st to first sc.

Rnd 24: Ch 1, sc in same st as joining and in next 5 sc, sc2tog, (sc in next 6 sc, sc2tog) around; join with slip st to first sc: 70 sc.

Rnds 25-27: Ch 1, sc in same st as joining and in each sc around; join with slip st to first sc.

Rnd 28: Ch 1, sc in same st as joining and in next 45 sc, place marker in last sc made for Flap and Trim placement, sc in each sc around; join with slip st to first sc, finish off.

Rnd 29: With **right** side facing, join Black with slip st in same st as joining; **loosely** slip st in each sc around; join with slip st to first slip st, finish off.

FLAP

Row 1: With **right** side facing and working in Back Loops Only, join Yellow with sc in marked st *(see Joining With Sc, page 46)*; do **not** remove marker, sc in next 29 sc, leave remaining sc unworked: 30 sc.

Rows 2-20: Ch 1, turn; sc in both loops of each sc across.

Rows 21 and 22: Turn; beginning in first sc, sc2tog, sc in each sc across to last 2 sc, sc2tog: 26 sc.

Finish off.

Trim: With **right** side facing, join Black with slip st in marked st, remove marker; sc in end of each row across Flap to last row, skip last row; beginning in first sc on last row, sc2tog, sc in each sc across to last 2 sc, sc2tog; skip first row, sc in end of each row across; slip st in same st as last sc on Row 1 of Flap, finish off.

WING (Make 2)

Rnd 1 (Right side)**:** With White, ch 2, 8 sc in second ch from hook; do **not** join, place marker to indicate beginning of rnd *(see Markers, page 46)*: 8 sc.

Rnd 2: 2 Sc in each sc around: 16 sc.

Rnd 3: (Sc in next sc, 2 sc in next sc) around: 24 sc.

Rnd 4: (Sc in next 2 sc, 2 sc in next sc) around: 32 sc.

Rnd 5: (Sc in next 3 sc, 2 sc in next sc) around: 40 sc.

Rnds 6-9: Sc in each sc around.

Rnd 10: (Sc2tog, sc in next 3 sc) around: 32 sc.

Rnd 11: (Sc2tog, sc in next 2 sc) around: 24 sc.

Rnd 12: (Sc2tog, sc in next sc) around: 16 sc.

Rnds 13 and 14: Sc in each sc around; at end of Rnd 14, slip st in next st, finish off leaving a long end for sewing.

EYE (Make 2)

Rnd 1 (Right side)**:** With Black, ch 4, 8 dc in fourth ch from hook; skip beginning ch and join with slip st to first dc: 8 dc.

Note: Mark Rnd 1 as **right** side.

Rnd 2: Ch 2, 2 dc in same st as joining and in each dc around; join with slip st to first dc, finish off: 16 dc.

Rnd 3: With **right** side facing, join White with sc in any dc; 2 sc in next dc, (sc in next dc, 2 sc in next dc) around; join with slip st to first sc, finish off leaving a long end for sewing.

Using photo on page 4 as a guide for placement, with White and straight stitch *(Fig. 5, page 47)*, add highlight to each Eye.

STRAP (Make 2)

With Black, ch 46, place marker in second ch from hook for st placement.

Rnd 1 (Right side)**:** Sc in second ch from hook and in each ch across to last ch, 3 sc in last ch; working in free loops of beginning ch, sc in each ch across to marked ch, 3 sc in marked ch, remove marker; join with slip st to first sc: 94 sc.

Note: Mark Rnd 1 as **right** side.

Rnd 2: Ch 1, sc in same st as joining and in each sc across to first 3-sc group, 3 sc in next sc, sc in next sc, 3 sc in next sc, sc in each sc across to next 3-sc group, 3 sc in next sc, sc in next sc, 3 sc in last sc; join with slip st to first sc, finish off leaving a long end for sewing.

FINISHING

Using photo as a guide for placement, long ends, and with **right** sides of all pieces facing:
Sew Eyes to Flap.
Sew Wings to sides of Body.
With Black and using straight stitch, add nose and mouth to Flap.

ANTENNA

With **right** side facing, join double strand of Black with slip st around fourth sc from edge of Flap and 3 rows above one Eye; ch 4, finish off. Trim ends.

Repeat for second Antenna.

Sew short end of each Strap to free loops of sts under Rnd 29 *(Fig. 2a, page 46)*, starting 5 sts from each edge of Flap. Sew remaining short end of each Strap to bottom edge of Body.
Glue hook-and-loop fastener circles to **wrong** side corners of Flap and to corresponding areas on Body.

●●○○ **EASY**

Finished Size:
15⅜" wide x 10" deep
(39 cm x 25.5 cm)

ALLIGATOR

Alligator
SHOPPING LIST

Yarn (Medium Weight)
[3.5 ounces, 170 yards
(100 grams, 156 meters) per skein]:
- ☐ Green - 2 skeins
- ☐ Tan - 1 skein
- ☐ White - 20 yards (18.5 meters)
- ☐ Yellow - 20 yards (18.5 meters)
- ☐ Black - small amount

Crochet Hook
- ☐ Size H (5 mm)
  or size needed for gauge

Additional Supplies
- ☐ ⅝" (16 mm) hook-and-loop fastener circles - 2
- ☐ Permanent fabric glue
- ☐ Yarn needle

GAUGE INFORMATION

13 sc and 13 rows = 4" (10 cm)
Gauge Swatch: 4" (10 cm) square
With Tan, ch 14.
Row 1: Sc in second ch from hook and in each ch across: 13 sc.
Rows 2-13: Ch 1, turn; sc in each sc across.
Finish off.

STITCH GUIDE

TREBLE CROCHET *(abbreviated tr)*
YO twice, insert hook in st indicated, YO and pull up a loop (4 loops on hook), (YO and draw through 2 loops on hook) 3 times.

SINGLE CROCHET 2 TOGETHER
   (abbreviated sc2tog)
Pull up a loop in each of next 2 sts, YO and draw through all 3 loops on hook (**counts as one sc**).

DOUBLE CROCHET 2 TOGETHER
   (abbreviated dc2tog)
   (uses next 2 sc)
★ YO, insert hook in **next** sc, YO and pull up a loop, YO and draw through 2 loops on hook; repeat from ★ once **more**, YO and draw through all 3 loops on hook (**counts as one dc**).

BASE

With Tan, ch 36.

Row 1 (Right side)**:** Sc in second ch from hook and in each ch across: 35 sc.

Note: Loop a short piece of yarn around any stitch to mark Row 1 as **right** side.

Rows 2-15: Ch 1, turn; sc in each sc across.

Do **not** finish off.

BODY

Rnd 1: Ch 1, do **not** turn; sc in end of each row across; working in free loops of beginning ch *(Fig. 2b, page 46)*, sc in each ch across; sc in end of each row across; sc in each sc across Row 15; join with slip st to Back Loop Only of first sc *(Fig. 1, page 46)*, finish off: 100 sc.

Rnd 2: With **right** side facing and working in Back Loops Only, join Green with sc in same st as joining *(see Joining With Sc, page 46)*; tr in next sc, (sc in next sc, tr in next sc) around; join with slip st to **both** loops of first sc.

Rnd 3: Ch 2 (**does not count as a st**), tr in same st as joining, sc in next tr, (tr in next sc, sc in next tr) around; join with slip st to first tr.

Rnd 4: Ch 1, sc in same st as joining, tr in next sc, (sc in next tr, tr in next sc) around; join with slip st to first sc.

Rnds 5-20: Repeat Rnds 3 and 4, 8 times.

Rnd 21: Ch 1, sc in same st as joining and in next 7 sts, sc2tog, (sc in next 8 sts, sc2tog) around; join with slip st to first sc: 90 sc.

Rnd 22: Ch 1, sc in same st as joining and in next 6 sc, sc2tog, (sc in next 7 sc, sc2tog) around; join with slip st to first sc: 80 sc.

Rnd 23: Ch 1, sc in same st as joining and in each sc around; join with slip st to first sc.

Rnd 24: Ch 1, sc in same st as joining and in next 5 sc, sc2tog, (sc in next 6 sc, sc2tog) around; join with slip st to first sc: 70 sc.

Rnds 25-27: Ch 1, sc in same st as joining and in each sc around; join with slip st to first sc.

Rnd 28: Ch 1, sc in same st as joining and in next 45 sc, place marker in last sc made for Flap and Trim placement, sc in each sc around; join with slip st to first sc, finish off.

FLAP

Row 1: With **right** side facing and working in Back Loops Only, join Green with sc in marked st; do **not** remove marker, sc in next 29 sc, leave remaining sc unworked: 30 sc.

Rows 2-20: Ch 1, turn; sc in both loops of each sc across.

Rows 21 and 22: Turn; beginning in first sc, sc2tog, sc in each sc across to last 2 sc, sc2tog: 26 sc.

Finish off.

Trim: With **right** side facing, join Green with slip st in marked st on Rnd 28, remove marker, sc in end of first 12 rows across Flap, place marker in last sc made for Teeth placement, sc in end of next 9 rows, skip last row; beginning in first sc on last row, sc2tog, sc in each sc across to last 2 sc, sc2tog; skip first row, sc in end of each row across; slip st in same st as last sc on Row 1 of Flap, finish off.

EYEBALL (Make 2)

Rnd 1 (Wrong side): With Yellow, ch 2, 4 sc in second ch from hook; do **not** join, place marker to indicate beginning of rnd *(see Markers, page 46)*.

Note: Mark the **back** of any sc on Rnd 1 as **right** side.

Rnd 2: 2 Sc in each sc around: 8 sc.

Rnds 3 and 4: Sc in each sc around.

Rnd 5: Sc2tog 4 times: 4 sc.

Turn Eyeball with **right** side facing, stuff with Yellow yarn; then sc2tog until hole is closed, finish off.

EYE SOCKET (Make 2)
With Green, ch 8.

Row 1: Sc in second ch from hook and in each ch across: 7 sc.

Rows 2 and 3: Ch 1, turn; sc in each sc across.

Row 4 (Right side)**:** Ch 1, turn; beginning in first sc, sc2tog, sc in next 3 sc, sc2tog: 5 sc.

Note: Mark Row 4 as **right** side.

Row 5: Ch 1, turn; sc in each sc across.

Row 6: Ch 1, turn; beginning in first sc, sc2tog, sc in next sc, sc2tog: 3 sc.

Trim: Ch 1, do **not** turn; sc in end of each row across to last row, 3 sc in end of last row; working in free loops of beginning ch, sc in each ch across; 3 sc in end of first row, sc in end of each row across; sc in each sc across last row; join with slip st to first sc, finish off leaving a long end for sewing.

TEETH
Row 1: With **right** side facing, join White with slip st in marked sc; ★ ch 1, dc2tog, ch 1, slip st in sp at top of dc2tog *(Fig. A)*, slip st in same sc as last leg of dc2tog; repeat from ★ 21 times **more**, finish off.

Fig. A

STRAP (Make 2)
With Tan, ch 46, place marker in second ch from hook for st placement.

Rnd 1 (Right side)**:** Sc in second ch from hook and in each ch across to last ch, 3 sc in last ch; working in free loops of beginning ch, sc in each ch across to marked ch, 3 sc in marked ch, remove marker; join with slip st to first sc: 94 sc.

Note: Mark Rnd 1 as **right** side.

Rnd 2: Ch 1, sc in same st as joining and in each sc across to first 3-sc group, 3 sc in next sc, sc in next sc, 3 sc in next sc, sc in each sc across to next 3-sc group, 3 sc in next sc, sc in next sc, 3 sc in last sc; join with slip st to first sc, finish off leaving a long end for sewing.

FINISHING
Using photo on page 26 as a guide to placement, long ends, and with **right** sides of all pieces facing:
With Black and using straight stitch *(Fig. 5, page 47)*, add pupil to each Eyeball across Rnds 1 and 2.
Sew Eye Socket around Eyeball and to Flap.
With Black and using straight stitch, add nostrils.
Sew short end of each Strap to free loops of sts on Rnd 28 *(Fig. 2a, page 46)*, starting 5 sts from each edge of Flap. Sew remaining short end of each Strap to bottom edge of Body.
Glue hook-and-loop fastener circles to **wrong** side corners of Flap and to corresponding areas on Body.

●●○○ **EASY**

Finished Size:
15⅜" wide x 10" deep
(39 cm x 25.5 cm)

SHOPPING LIST

Yarn (Medium Weight) 🧶**4**

[3.5 ounces, 170 yards
(100 grams, 156 meters) per skein]:

☐ Grey - 2 skeins

☐ Green - 1 skein

☐ Blue - 1 skein

☐ White - 1 skein

☐ Black - 10 yards (9 meters)

Crochet Hook

☐ Size H (5 mm)

or size needed for gauge

Additional Supplies

☐ Safety pin

☐ ⅝" (16 mm) hook-and-loop
fastener circles - 2

☐ Permanent fabric glue

☐ Polyester fiberfill

☐ Yarn needle

DINO

Dino

GAUGE INFORMATION

13 sc and 13 rows = 4" (10 cm)

Gauge Swatch: 4" (10 cm) square
With White, ch 14.

Row 1: Sc in second ch from hook
and in each ch across: 13 sc.

Rows 2-13: Ch 1, turn; sc in each sc
across.
Finish off.

STITCH GUIDE

SINGLE CROCHET 2 TOGETHER
(abbreviated sc2tog)

Pull up a loop in each of next 2 sts,
YO and draw through all 3 loops on
hook (**counts as one sc**).

BASE

With Green, ch 36.

Row 1 (Right side)**:** Sc in second ch
from hook and in each ch across:
35 sc.

Note: Loop a short piece of yarn
around any stitch to mark Row 1 as
right side.

Rows 2-15: Ch 1, turn; sc in each sc
across.

Do **not** finish off.

BODY

Rnd 1: Ch 1, do **not** turn; sc in end
of each row across; working in free
loops of beginning ch (*Fig. 2b,
page 46*), sc in each ch across; sc in
end of each row across; sc in each
sc across Row 15; join with slip st
to Back Loop Only of first sc (*Fig. 1,
page 46*), finish off: 100 sc.

Work in Back Loops Only through
Rnd 37.

Rnd 2: With **right** side facing; join
Blue with sc in same st as joining (*see
Joining With Sc, page 46*); sc in each
sc around; join with slip st to first
sc, do **not** finish off, place loop from
hook onto safety pin to keep piece
from unraveling while working the
next rnd.

Rnd 3: With **right** side facing, join
Grey with sc in same st as joining; sc
in each sc around; join with slip st to
first sc, finish off.

Rnd 4: Remove loop from safety
pin and place on hook. Ch 1, sc in
same st as joining and in each sc
around; join with slip st to first sc,
do **not** finish off, place loop from
hook onto safety pin to keep piece
from unraveling while working the
next rnd.

Rnd 5: With Green, repeat Rnd 3.

Rnd 6: Repeat Rnd 4.

Rnds 7-9: Repeat Rnds 3-5.

Rnd 10: Remove loop from safety pin
and place on hook. Ch 1, sc in same
st as joining and in each sc around;
join with slip st to first sc, finish off.

Rnd 11: With **right** side facing, join
Grey with sc in same st as joining; sc
in each sc around; do **not** join, place
marker to indicate beginning of rnd
(*see Markers, page 46*).

Rnds 12-30: Sc in each sc around.

Rnd 31: (Sc in next 8 sc, sc2tog)
around: 90 sc.

Rnd 32: (Sc in next 7 sc, sc2tog)
around: 80 sc.

Rnd 33: Sc in each sc around.

Rnd 34: (Sc in next 6 sc, sc2tog)
around: 70 sc.

Rnds 35-37: Sc in each sc around; at
end of Rnd 37, slip st in **both** loops of
next sc, finish off.

Rnd 38: With **right** side facing and
working in both loops, join Blue with
sc in same st as slip st; sc in next
45 sc, place marker in last sc made for
Flap and Trim placement, sc in each
sc around; join with slip st to first sc,
finish off.

FLAP

Row 1: With **right** side facing and working in Back Loops Only, join Grey with sc in marked st; do **not** remove marker, sc in next 29 sc, leave remaining sc unworked: 30 sc.

Rows 2-20: Ch 1, turn; sc in both loops of each sc across.

Rows 21 and 22: Turn; beginning in first sc, sc2tog, sc in each sc across to last 2 sc, sc2tog: 26 sc.

Finish off.

Trim: With **right** side facing, join Blue with slip st in marked st, remove marker; sc in end of each row across Flap to last row, skip last row; beginning in first sc on last row, sc2tog, sc in next 5 sc, place marker in last sc made for Muzzle placement, sc in each sc across to last 2 sc, sc2tog; skip first row, sc in end of each row across; slip st in same st as last sc on Row 1 of Flap, finish off.

LARGE SPIKE

Rnd 1 (Right side)**:** With White, ch 2, 3 sc in second ch from hook; do **not** join, place marker to indicate beginning of rnd.

Note: Mark Rnd 1 as **right** side.

Rnd 2: 2 Sc in each sc around: 6 sc.

Rnd 3: Sc in each sc around.

Rnd 4: (Sc in next sc, 2 sc in next sc) around: 9 sc.

Rnd 5: Sc in each sc around.

Rnd 6: (Sc in next 2 sc, sc in next 2 sc) around: 12 sc.

Rnds 7-10: Sc in each sc around; at end of Rnd 10, slip st in next sc, finish off leaving a long end for sewing.

Stuff Large Spike with polyester fiberfill.

MEDIUM SPIKE (Make 2)

Rnds 1-7: Work same as Large Spike; at end of Rnd 7, slip st in next sc, finish off leaving a long end for sewing: 12 sc.

Stuff Medium Spike with polyester fiberfill.

SMALL SPIKE

Rnds 1-5: Work same as Large Spike; at end of Rnd 5, slip st in next sc, finish off leaving a long end for sewing: 9 sc.

Stuff Small Spike with polyester fiberfill.

EYE (Make 2)

Rnd 1 (Right side)**:** With Black, ch 2, 5 sc in second ch from hook; join with slip st to first sc.

Note: Mark Rnd 1 as **right** side.

Rnd 2: Ch 1, 2 sc in same st as joining and in each sc around; join with slip st to first sc, finish off leaving a long end for sewing.

Using photo on page 30 as a guide for placement, with White and straight stitch (*Fig. 5, page 47*), add highlight to each Eye.

MUZZLE

Row 1: With **right** side facing and working Front Loops Only, join Green with sc in marked st on Flap Trim, remove marker; sc in next 16 sc, leave remaining sc unworked: 17 sc.

Rows 2-7: Ch 1, turn; sc in both loops of each sc across.

Rows 8-11: Ch 1, turn; beginning in first sc, sc2tog, sc across to last 2 sc, sc2tog: 9 sc.

Finish off leaving a long end for sewing.

Sew Muzzle to Flap. With White and using straight st, add 'X' nostrils to Muzzle.

LARGE SPOT

(Make one **each** with Green and Blue)

Rnd 1 (Right side)**:** Ch 4, 10 dc in fourth ch from hook; skip beginning ch and join with slip st to first dc.

Note: Mark Rnd 1 as **right** side.

Rnd 2: Ch 2 (**does not count as a st, now and throughout**), 2 dc in same st as joining and in each dc around; join with slip st to first dc: 20 dc.

Rnd 3: Ch 2, dc in same st as joining, 2 dc in next dc, (dc in next dc, 2 dc in next dc) around; join with slip st to first dc, finish off leaving a long end for sewing.

MEDIUM SPOT

(Make one **each** with Green and Blue)

Rnds 1 and 2: Work same as Large Spot: 20 dc.

Finish off leaving a long end for sewing.

SMALL SPOT

(Make one **each** with Green and Blue)

Rnd 1 (Right side)**:** Ch 4, 10 dc in fourth ch from hook; skip beginning ch and join with slip st to first dc, finish off leaving a long end for sewing.

STRAP (Make 2)

With Blue, ch 46, place marker in second ch from hook for st placement.

Rnd 1 (Right side)**:** Sc in second ch from hook and in each ch across to last ch, 3 sc in last ch; working in free loops of beginning ch, sc in each ch across to marked ch, 3 sc in marked ch, remove marker; join with slip st to first sc: 94 sc.

Note: Mark Rnd 1 as **right** side.

Rnd 2: Ch 1, sc in same st as joining and in each sc across to first 3-sc group, 3 sc in next sc, sc in next sc, 3 sc in next sc, sc in each sc across to next 3-sc group, 3 sc in next sc, sc in next sc, 3 sc in last sc; join with slip st to first sc, finish off leaving a long end for sewing.

FINISHING

Using photo as a guide for placement, long ends, and with **right** sides of all pieces facing:
Sew Eyes to Flap.

Sew short end of each Strap to free loops of sts on Rnd 38 *(Fig. 2a, page 46)*, starting 5 sts from each edge of Flap. Sew remaining short end of each Strap to bottom edge of Body.
Glue hook-and-loop fastener circles to **wrong** side corners of Flap and to corresponding areas on Body.
Sew Spots to Body as desired.
Sew Small Spike to center of Muzzle.
Centering Large Spike to middle of Rnd 38 between Straps, sew Large Spike to first 2 rows of Flap and last 2 rnds of Body; then sew one Medium Spike to each side of Large Spike spacing 2 sc apart.

●●○○ EASY

Finished Size:
15⅜" wide x 10" deep
(39 cm x 25.5 cm)

PANDA

Panda

SHOPPING LIST

Yarn (Medium Weight) 🔠4🔠
[7 ounces, 370 yards
(198 grams, 338 meters) per skein]:

☐ Red - 1 skein
☐ White - 1 skein
☐ Black - 1 skein

Crochet Hook
☐ Size H (5 mm)
or size needed for gauge

Additional Supplies
☐ ⅝" (16 mm) hook-and-loop
fastener circles - 2
☐ Permanent fabric glue
☐ Yarn needle

GAUGE INFORMATION
13 sc and 13 rows = 4" (10 cm)
Gauge Swatch: 4" (10 cm) square
With Red, ch 14.
Row 1: Sc in second ch from hook
and in each ch across: 13 sc.
Rows 2-13: Ch 1, turn; sc in each sc
across.
Finish off.

STITCH GUIDE
SINGLE CROCHET 2 TOGETHER
(abbreviated sc2tog)
Pull up a loop in each of next 2 sts,
YO and draw through all 3 loops on
hook (**counts as one sc**).

BASE
With Red, ch 36.

Row 1 (Right side): Sc in second ch
from hook and in each ch across:
35 sc.

Note: Loop a short piece of yarn
around any stitch to mark Row 1 as
right side.

Rows 2-15: Ch 1, turn; sc in each sc
across.

Do **not** finish off.

BODY
Rnd 1: Ch 1, do **not** turn; sc in end
of each row across; working in free
loops of beginning ch *(Fig. 2b,
page 46)*, sc in each ch across; sc in
end of each row across; sc in each
sc across Row 15; join with slip st
to Back Loop Only of first sc *(Fig. 1,
page 46)*: 100 sc.

Rnd 2: Ch 1, sc in Back Loop Only
of same st as joining and each sc
around; join with slip st to **both** loops
of first sc.

Rnd 3: Ch 1, sc in both loops of same
st as joining and in each sc around;
do **not** join, place marker to indicate
beginning of rnd *(see Markers,
page 46)*.

Rnds 4-30: Sc in each sc around; at
end of Rnd 30, slip st in next sc.

Rnd 31: Ch 1, sc in same st as slip st
and in next 7 sc, sc2tog, (sc in next
8 sc, sc2tog) around; join with slip st
to first sc: 90 sc.

Rnd 32: Ch 1, sc in same st as joining
and in next 6 sc, sc2tog, (sc in next
7 sc, sc2tog) around; join with slip st
to first sc: 80 sc.

Rnd 33: Ch 1, sc in same st as joining
and in each sc around; join with
slip st to first sc.

Rnd 34: Ch 1, sc in same st as joining
and in next 5 sc, sc2tog, (sc in next
6 sc, sc2tog) around; join with slip st
to first sc: 70 sc.

Rnds 35 and 36: Ch 1, sc in same st
as joining and in each sc around; join
with slip st to first sc.

Finish off.

Rnd 37: With **right** side facing, join
Black with sc in same st as joining
(see Joining With Sc, page 46); sc in
each sc around; join with slip st to
first sc.

Rnd 38: Ch 1, sc in same st as joining
and in next 50 sc, place marker in last
sc made for Flap and Trim placement,
sc in each sc around; join with slip st
to first sc, finish off.

FLAP

Row 1: With **right** side facing and working in Back Loops Only, join Black with sc in marked st; do **not** remove marker, sc in next 29 sc, leave remaining sc unworked: 30 sc.

Row 2: Ch 1, turn; sc in both loops of each sc across; finish off.

Row 3: With **right** side facing, join White with sc in first sc; sc in each sc across.

Rows 4-20: Ch 1, turn; sc in each sc across.

Rows 21 and 22: Turn; beginning in first sc, sc2tog, sc in each sc across to last 2 sc, sc2tog: 26 sc.

Finish off.

Trim: With **right** side facing, join Black with slip st in marked st on Rnd 38, remove marker; sc in end of each row across Flap to last row, skip last row; beginning in first sc on last row, sc2tog, sc in each sc across to last 2 sc, sc2tog; skip first row, sc in end of each row across; slip st in same st as last sc on Row 1 of Flap, finish off.

FIRST EYE PATCH

Row 1: With Black, ch 4, 2 sc in second ch from hook, 3 sc in last ch: 5 sc.

Row 2: Ch 1, turn; 2 sc in first sc, sc in next 3 sc, 2 sc in last sc: 7 sc.

Row 3: Ch 1, turn; sc in each sc across.

Row 4: Ch 1, turn; beginning in first sc, sc2tog, sc in each sc across: 6 sc.

Row 5: Ch 1, turn; sc in first 4 sc, sc2tog: 5 sc.

Rows 6-9: Ch 1, turn; sc in each sc across.

Row 10: Ch 1, turn; beginning in first sc, sc2tog, sc in next sc, sc2tog: 3 sc.

Row 11: Ch 1, turn; beginning in first sc, sc2tog, pulling up a loop in same st and in last sc, sc2tog; do **not** finish off: 2 sc.

Trim (Right side)**:** Ch 1, turn; sc evenly around Eye Patch; join with slip st to first sc, finish off leaving a long end for sewing.

Note: Mark Trim as **right** side.

SECOND EYE PATCH

Rows 1-11: Work same as First Eye Patch: 2 sc.

Trim (Right side)**:** Ch 1, do **not** turn; sc evenly around Eye Patch; join with slip st to first sc, finish off leaving a long end for sewing.

Note: Mark Trim as **right** side.

Using photo on page 36 as a guide for placement, with White and straight stitch *(Fig. 5, page 47)*, add highlight to each Eye Patch.

EAR (Make 2)

Rnd 1 (Right side)**:** With Black, ch 2, 5 sc in second ch from hook; do **not** join, place marker to indicate beginning of rnd.

Rnd 2: 2 Sc in each sc around: 10 sc.

Rnd 3: (Sc in next sc, 2 sc in next sc) around: 15 sc.

Rnds 4 and 5: Sc in each sc around.

Rnd 6: (Sc in next sc, sc2tog) around; slip st in next sc, finish off leaving a long end for sewing.

STRAP (Make 2)

With Black, ch 46, place marker in second ch from hook for st placement.

Rnd 1 (Right side): Sc in second ch from hook and in each ch across to last ch, 3 sc in last ch; working in free loops of beginning ch, sc in each ch across to marked ch, 3 sc in marked ch, remove marker; join with slip st to first sc: 94 sc.

Note: Mark Rnd 1 as **right** side.

Rnd 2: Ch 1, sc in same st as joining and in each sc across to first 3-sc group, 3 sc in next sc, sc in next sc, 3 sc in next sc, sc in each sc across to next 3-sc group, 3 sc in next sc, sc in next sc, 3 sc in last sc; join with slip st to first sc, finish off leaving a long end for sewing.

FINISHING

Using photo as a guide for placement, long ends, and with **right** sides of all pieces facing:
Sew each Eye Patch to Flap.
Sew each Ear at a slight angle across top corners of Flap.
With Black and using satin stitch *(Figs. 4a & b, page 47)*, add nose.

Sew short end of each Strap to free loops of sts on Rnd 38 *(Fig. 2a, page 46)*, starting 5 sts from each edge of Flap. Sew remaining short end of each Strap to bottom edge of Body.
Glue hook-and-loop fastener circles to **wrong** side corners of Flap and to corresponding areas on Body.

● ● ○ ○ **EASY**

Finished Size:
15³⁄₈" wide x 10" deep
(39 cm x 25.5 cm)

SHOPPING LIST

Yarn (Medium Weight) 🧶**4**
[3.5 ounces, 170 yards
(100 grams, 156 meters) per skein]:

☐ Grey - 2 skeins

☐ Red - 1 skein

☐ White - 1 skein

☐ Black - 10 yards (9 meters)

Crochet Hook

☐ Size H (5 mm)

or size needed for gauge

Additional Supplies

☐ ⁵⁄₈" (16 mm) hook-and-loop
fastener circles - 2

☐ Permanent fabric glue

☐ Yarn needle

SOCK MONKEY

Sock Monkey

GAUGE INFORMATION

13 sc and 13 rows = 4" (10 cm)

Gauge Swatch: 4" (10 cm) square

With White, ch 14.

Row 1: Sc in second ch from hook and in each ch across: 13 sc.

Rows 2-13: Ch 1, turn; sc in each sc across.

Finish off.

STITCH GUIDE

SINGLE CROCHET 2 TOGETHER

(abbreviated sc2tog)

Pull up a loop in each of next 2 sts, YO and draw through all 3 loops on hook **(counts as one sc)**.

BASE

With Grey, ch 36.

Row 1 (Right side)**:** Sc in second ch from hook and in each ch across: 35 sc.

Note: Loop a short piece of yarn around any stitch to mark Row 1 as **right** side.

Rows 2-15: Ch 1, turn; sc in each sc across.

Do **not** finish off.

BODY

Rnd 1: Ch 1, do **not** turn; sc in end of each row across; working in free loops of beginning ch *(Fig. 2b, page 46)*, sc in each ch across; sc in end of each row across; sc in each sc across Row 15; join with slip st to Back Loop Only of first sc *(Fig. 1, page 46)*: 100 sc.

Rnd 2: Ch 2 **(does not count as a st, now and throughout)**, working in Back Loops Only, dc in same st as joining and in each sc around; join with slip st to **both** loops of first dc.

Rnds 3-14: Ch 2, working in both loops, dc in same st as joining and in each dc around; join with slip st to first dc.

Finish off.

Rnd 15: With **right** side facing, join Red with sc in same st as joining *(see Joining With Sc, page 46)*; sc in next 7 dc, sc2tog, (sc in next 8 dc, sc2tog) around; join with slip st to first sc: 90 sc.

Rnd 16: Ch 1, sc in same st as joining and in next 6 sc, sc2tog, (sc in next 7 sc, sc2tog) around; join with slip st to first sc, finish off: 80 sc.

Rnd 17: With **right** side facing, join White with sc in same st as joining; sc in each sc around; join with slip st to first sc.

Rnd 18: Ch 1, sc in same st as joining and in next 5 sc, sc2tog, (sc in next 6 sc, sc2tog) around; join with slip st to first sc: 70 sc.

Rnds 19-21: Ch 1, sc in same st as joining and in each sc around; join with slip st to first sc.

Rnd 22: Ch 1, sc in same st as joining and in next 48 sc, place marker in last sc made for Flap and Trim placement, sc in each sc around; join with slip st to first sc, finish off.

FLAP

Row 1: With **right** side facing and working in Back Loops Only, join White with sc in marked st; do **not** remove marker, sc in next 29 sc, leave remaining sc unworked: 30 sc.

Rows 2-6: Ch 1, turn; sc in both loops of each sc across.

Finish off.

Row 7: With **right** side facing, join Red with sc in first sc; sc in each sc across.

Row 8: Ch 1, turn; sc in each sc across; finish off.

Row 9: With **right** side facing, join Grey with sc in first sc; sc in each sc across.

Rows 10-20: Ch 1, turn; sc in each sc across.

Rows 21 and 22: Turn; beginning in first sc, sc2tog, sc in each sc across to last 2 sc, sc2tog: 26 sc.

Finish off.

Trim: With **right** side facing, join Grey with slip st in marked st on Rnd 22, remove marker; sc in end of each row across Flap to last row, skip last row; beginning in first sc on last row, sc2tog, sc in each sc across to last 2 sc, sc2tog; skip first row, sc in end of each row across; slip st in same st as last sc on Row 1 of Flap, finish off.

EYE (Make 2)

Rnd 1 (Right side)**:** With Black, ch 2, 5 sc in second ch from hook; join with slip st to first sc

Note: Mark Rnd 1 as **right** side.

Rnd 2: Ch 1, 2 sc in same st as joining and in each sc around; join with slip st to first sc, finish off leaving a long end for sewing.

MUZZLE

With White, ch 21.

Rnd 1 (Right side): 3 Dc in fourth ch from hook (**3 skipped chs count as first dc**), dc in each ch across to last ch, 4 dc in last ch; working in free loops of beginning ch, dc in next 16 chs; join with slip st to first dc, finish off leaving a long end for sewing.

With two strands of Red and using backstitch (**Fig. 3, page 47**), add mouth across beginning ch of Muzzle.

STRAP (Make 2)

With Grey, ch 46, place marker in second ch from hook for st placement.

Rnd 1 (Right side)**:** Sc in second ch from hook and in each ch across to last ch, 3 sc in last ch; working in free loops of beginning ch, sc in each ch across to marked ch, 3 sc in marked ch, remove marker; join with slip st to first sc: 94 sc.

Note: Mark Rnd 1 as **right** side.

Rnd 2: Ch 1, sc in same st as joining and in each sc across to first 3-sc group, 3 sc in next sc, sc in next sc, 3 sc in next sc, sc in each sc across to next 3-sc group, 3 sc in next sc, sc in next sc, 3 sc in last sc; join with slip st to first sc, finish off leaving a long end for sewing.

FINISHING

Using photo on page 40 as a guide for placement, long ends, and with **right** sides of all pieces facing: Sew Eyes and Muzzle to Flap. Sew short end of each Strap to free loops of sts on Rnd 22 (**Fig. 2a, page 46**), starting 5 sts from each edge of Flap. Sew remaining short end of each Strap to bottom edge of Body.

Glue hook-and-loop fastener circles to **wrong** side corners of Flap and to corresponding areas on Body.

POM-POM

Cut a piece of cardboard 3" (7.5 cm) square.

Wind the yarn around the cardboard until it is approximately ½" (12 mm) thick in the middle (**Fig. A**).

Carefully slip the yarn off the cardboard and firmly tie an 18" (45.5 cm) length of yarn around the middle (**Fig. B**). Leave yarn ends long enough to attach the pom-pom. Cut the loops on both ends and trim the pom-pom into a smooth ball (**Fig. C**).

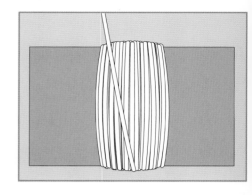

Fig. A

Fig. B

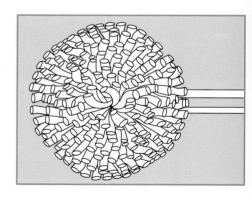

Fig. C

Sew pom-pom to center of Row 1 on Flap.

General Instructions

ABBREVIATIONS

ch(s)	chain(s)
cm	centimeters
dc	double crochet(s)
dc2tog	double crochet 2 together
LSC	Long Single Crochet(s)
mm	millimeters
Rnd(s)	Round(s)
sc	single crochet(s)
sc2tog	single crochet 2 together
sp(s)	space(s)
st(s)	stitch(es)
tr	treble crochet(s)
YO	yarn over

SYMBOLS & TERMS

★ — work instructions following ★ as many **more** times as indicated in addition to the first time.

† to † — work all instructions from first † to † second **as many** times as specified.

( ) or [ ] — work enclosed instructions **as many** times as specified by the number immediately following **or** work all enclosed instructions in the stitch or space indicated **or** contains explanatory remarks.

colon (:) — the number(s) given after a colon at the end of a row or round denote(s) the number of stitches and spaces you should have on that row or round.

GAUGE

Exact gauge is **essential** for proper size. Before beginning your Backpack, make the sample swatch given in the individual instructions in the yarn and hook specified. After completing the swatch, measure it, counting your stitches and rows carefully. If your swatch is larger or smaller than specified, **make another, changing hook size to get the correct gauge**. Keep trying until you find the size hook that will give you the specified gauge.

CROCHET TERMINOLOGY	
UNITED STATES	INTERNATIONAL
slip stitch (slip st) =	single crochet (sc)
single crochet (sc) =	double crochet (dc)
half double crochet (hdc) =	half treble crochet (htr)
double crochet (dc) =	treble crochet (tr)
treble crochet (tr) =	double treble crochet (dtr)
double treble crochet (dtr) =	triple treble crochet (ttr)
triple treble crochet (tr tr) =	quadruple treble crochet (qtr)
skip =	miss

Yarn Weight Symbol & Names	LACE 0	SUPER FINE 1	FINE 2	LIGHT 3	MEDIUM 4	BULKY 5	SUPER BULKY 6	JUMBO 7
Type of Yarns in Category	Fingering, size 10 crochet thread	Sock, Fingering, Baby	Sport, Baby	DK, Light Worsted	Worsted, Afghan, Aran	Chunky, Craft, Rug	Super Bulky, Roving	Jumbo, Roving
Crochet Gauge* Ranges in Single Crochet to 4" (10 cm)	32-42 sts**	21-32 sts	16-20 sts	12-17 sts	11-14 sts	8-11 sts	6-9 sts	5 sts and fewer
Advised Hook Size Range	Steel*** 6 to 8, Regular hook B-1	B-1 to E-4	E-4 to 7	7 to I-9	I-9 to K-10½	K-10½ to M/N-13	M/N-13 to Q	Q and larger

*GUIDELINES ONLY: The chart above reflects the most commonly used gauges and hook sizes for specific yarn categories.

** Lace weight yarns are usually crocheted with larger hooks to create lacy openwork patterns. Accordingly, a gauge range is difficult to determine. Always follow the gauge stated in your pattern.

*** Steel crochet hooks are sized differently from regular hooks–the higher the number, the smaller the hook, which is the reverse of regular hook sizing.

MARKERS

Markers are used to help distinguish the beginning of each round being worked. Place a 2" (5 cm) scrap piece of yarn before the first stitch of each round, moving marker after each round is complete.

JOINING WITH SC

When instructed to join with sc, begin with a slip knot on hook. Insert hook in stitch or space indicated, YO and pull up a loop, YO and draw through both loops on hook.

JOINING WITH DC

When instructed to join with dc, begin with a slip knot on hook. YO, holding loop on hook, insert hook in stitch or space indicated, YO and pull up a loop (3 loops on hook), (YO and draw through 2 loops on hook) twice.

BACK OR FRONT LOOP ONLY

Work only in loop(s) indicated by arrow *(Fig. 1)*.

Fig. 1

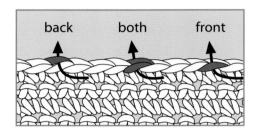

FREE LOOPS

After working in Back or Front Loops Only on a row or round, there will be a ridge of unused loops. These are called the free loops. Later, when instructed to work in the free loops of the same row or round, work in these loops *(Fig. 2a)*.
When instructed to work in free loops of a chain, work in loop indicated by arrow *(Fig. 2b)*.

Fig. 2a

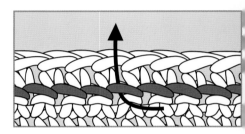

Fig. 2b

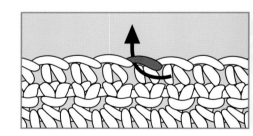

CROCHET HOOKS																
U.S.	B-1	C-2	D-3	E-4	F-5	G-6	7	H-8	I-9	J-10	K-10½	L-11	M/N-13	N/P-15	P/Q	Q	S
Metric - mm	2.25	2.75	3.25	3.5	3.75	4	4.5	5	5.5	6	6.5	8	9	10	15	16	19

●○○○ **BEGINNER**	Projects for first-time crocheters using basic stitches. Minimal shaping.
●●○○ **EASY**	Projects using yarn with basic stitches, repetitive stitch patterns, simple color changes, and simple shaping and finishing.
●●●○ **INTERMEDIATE**	Projects using a variety of techniques, such as basic lace patterns or color patterns, mid-level shaping and finishing.
●●●● **EXPERIENCED**	Projects with intricate stitch patterns, techniques and dimension, such as non-repeating patterns, multi-color techniques, fine threads, small hooks, detailed shaping and refined finishing.

Embroidery Stitches

BACKSTITCH

Backstitch is worked from **right** to **left**. Come up at 1, go down at 2 and come up at 3 *(Fig. 3)*. The second stitch is made by going down at 1 and coming up at 4.

Fig. 3

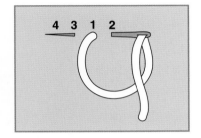

SATIN STITCH

Satin stitch is a series of straight stitches worked side-by-side so they touch but do not overlap *(Fig. 4a)* **or** come out of and go into the same stitches *(Fig. 4b)*. Come up at odd numbers and go down at even numbers.

Fig. 4a

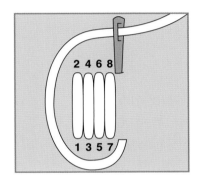

Fig. 4b

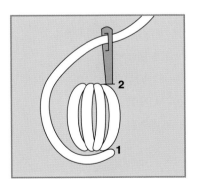

STRAIGHT STITCH

Straight stitch is just what the name implies, a single, straight stitch. Come up at 1 and go down at 2 *(Fig. 5)*.

Fig. 5

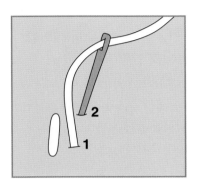

Yarn Information

Each Backpack in this book was made using Medium Weight Yarn. Any brand of Medium Weight Yarn may be used. It is best to refer to the yardage/meters when determining how many balls or skeins to purchase. Remember, to arrive at the finished size, it is the GAUGE/TENSION that is important, not the brand of yarn.

For your convenience, listed below are the specific yarns used to create our photography models. Because yarn manufacturers make frequent changes to their product lines, you may sometimes find it necessary to use a substitute yarn or to search for the discontinued product at alternate suppliers (locally or online).

GIRAFFE
Red Heart® With Love®
Gold - #1207 Cornsilk
Brown - #1321 Chocolate
Off White - #1303 Aran
Black - #1012 Black
White - #1001 White

LION
Lion Brand® Vanna's Choice®
Beige - #123 Beige
Brown - #125 Taupe
Blue - #109 Colonial Blue
Black - #153 Black
White - #100 White

ZEBRA
Red Heart® With Love®
Pink - #1701 Hot Pink
White - #1001 White
Black - #1012 Black

BEE
Red Heart® With Love®
Yellow - #1201 Daffodil
Black - #1012 Black
White - #1001 White

ALLIGATOR
Lion Brand® Vanna's Choice®
Green - #173 Dusty Green
Tan - #099 Linen
White - #100 White
Yellow - #159 Lemon
Black - #153 Black

DINO
Lion Brand® Vanna's Choice®
Grey - #150 Pale Grey
Green - #172 Kelly Green
Blue - #109 Colonial Blue
White - #100 White
Black - #153 Black

PANDA
Red Heart® With Love®
Red - #1909 Holly Berry
White - #1001 White
Black - #1012 Black

SOCK MONKEY
Lion Brand® Vanna's Choice®
Grey - #149 Silver Grey
Red - #113 Scarlet
White - #100 White
Black - #153 Black

We have made every effort to ensure that these instructions are accurate and complete. We cannot, however, be responsible for human error, typographical mistakes, or variations in individual work.

Production Team: Instructional/ Technical Editor - Sarah J. Green; Senior Graphic Artist - Lora Puls; Graphic Artist - Amy L. Teeter; Photo Stylist - Lori Wenger; and Photographer - Jason Masters.